THE REIGN OF SPARROWS

By the same author

Poetry
Collected Poems 1936–61
Buff
New Poems
Tiny Tears
From the Joke Shop

Novels
With My Little Eye
The Second Curtain
Fantasy and Fugue
Image of a Society
The Ruined Boys
The Father's Comedy
The Perfect Fool
My Child, My Sister
The Carnal Island

Criticism
Owls and Artificers
Professors and Gods

ROY FULLER

The Reign of Sparrows

LONDON MAGAZINE EDITIONS 1980

Published by London Magazine Editions
30 Thurloe Place, London, S.W.7

© Roy Fuller 1980
SBN 904388 29 8

Printed by
Unwin Brothers Limited,
The Gresham Press,
Old Woking, Surrey

To Alan Ross

CONTENTS

Two Muses 9
Ghost Voice 11
Saints and Stoics 14
The Sloth Moth 18
Musical Offering 18
Hedge-sparrows and House-sparrows 23
On His Sixtieth Birthday 23
Dreamless Night 26
Visiting the Great 28
Cinquains 29
School Time, Work Time 33
Oxford Album 33
Notebook 34
Two Blond Flautists 34
140 Years On 35
On Birkett Marshall's *Rare Poems of the Seventeenth Century* 37
1935–75 38
Autumnal Metamorphoses 39
Crisis 40
The Old Toy 41
In His Sixty-fifth Year 41
Voluminous Art, Short Life 48
Shop Talk 49
Quatrains of an Elderly Man 50
On His Sixty-fifth Birthday 54
Buckland's *Curiosities of Natural History* 58
Morning 59
Aberdeen Revisited 60
Old Poets 61
The Life of the Bee 61
Last Dreams 63
Devilish Times 64
To George Woodcock, in His and the Author's Sixty-fifth Year 66
Notes 69

TWO MUSES

Just as I thought that death could never end
Evenings of aqua-vitae, writing verse,
So I ignored the Spartan lust to lead
The League – and found myself in Spartan jails.

Or, rather, only too keenly felt the threat
Of that displeasing ideology!
It haunted my quiet felicity as much
As expectation of a drawn-out death.

Sunsets were never smug: witness my odes.
The life not uniformly contemplative:
See, in my souvenirs, the years when I
Was quartermaster to the Seventh Horse.

And yet the element of self-delusion
Asserted itself so often one might think
It was in human nature to be calm;
To be united, human destiny.

Who could have summoned up his naked child
Running along some road, her back on fire?
He would have surely told himself: 'Before
That stage the rules of folly will have changed.'

A memory rises of the former war:
One of our stallions, upper lip retracted,
Its somewhat rubbery implement unsheathed,
Alarmingly trumpeting with so-called love.

Awed by the frenzied drive yet pitying
The creature in its toils, I wondered if
The joined and slanting teeth were pincering
The filly's neck in rage or tenderness.

And wondered whether to be safe from force
Would have to be installed a matriarchy.
Now in my less erotic years I see
Fathers are selfless, too. And mothers . . . well.

Touching that jailors sometimes still appear
To belong to the human species: though who can tell
The significance of that? Conviction veers
Between condemning Nature and the State.

Thrusting tin plates of beans before your nose,
They say: 'We sang your songs on windy plains.'
Doubtful. They say that slumber is forbidden –
Rather more like the men of will they are.

That women can be aggressive, too, is known
By comics and benedicts. Children grow to hate
Or ridicule the customs of the nest,
Even the clever artifact itself.

Still, they must improvise their own in time.
Still, we've no hope but that of creature love –
Which the deformed give most, the very ones
Sparta leaves out to perish on its hills.

They said: 'You're an early number in our book.
We took you over from your own lot's list.'
Precisely: were they wise, states and their brass
Need only murder us and not each other.

Artists imagine that they serve the nation –
Mostly against its will. My case: preventing
A few from being shot. The relevant
Passages weren't made much of by my class.

It little matters I remain obscure;
I've had so much from poetry and life.
Can't even care about posterity's
Possible benison. Dear jailors, go

Off duty to live those lives you think secure;
Torture your children mildly and your wives
And get what comfort comes from leisure time
And being for a little while top dogs.

The plate, once symbol of advancing culture –
Ore that drew travellers to dusty lands:
I dream of making arms of it again,
As though its limpness might defeat the bronze.

As though such counter-violence, being weak,
Could be excused. As though the chanting Muse
Were forced to bear the obnoxious duties of
Her suffering eldest sister, History.

GHOST VOICE

    1

We're in the second phase
Of my truancy. At first
Your grief seemed merely designed
To prove my virtue: for me
The greatest sacrifice
Giving up the everyday.
But now I almost enjoy
This liberty bizarre:
Responsibilities gone
I'd forgotten were tyrannies;
Even no need to fret
About your diurnal tears.

And I see you too have changed
Your habits: freedom has come
To draw on my estate,
To let out a social sob,
To sketch another life –
Effaced, the desire at my death
To be absent for ever yourself.

      2

Like you, we absentees with certainty
Can't meet the lost ones of our former lives.
And yet we see more clearly that they form,
With us, a whole confederacy of truth.
For in our novel state they'll never be
Forgotten, as they are in your sad world –
Often by dwindling agents of remembrance.
Scarcely-named siblings, dead in babyhood,
Are here recalled, with visionary force
Now the design's last curlicue is traced.
And, our disguises left behind (spies' hats,
Executive flannel and retired man's slacks,
Each offering a problem of disposal),
Play-acting is no longer possible.
But we suppose you well aware of that
Since our rhetorical gestures of farewell –
Odes, epitaphs, that moved you, though drawn up
By the still-alive – have now been really made.

3

I seem to hear you say
'Don't make too strenuous
An effort to return.'
Are you afraid to have
To live with terminal
Disease a second time
Or that you envisage
The graveyard's further ravage
Of the slight thickness on
The bone, that held your love?

Or has your loss already
Changed to a kind of art
Where the obtrusion of
A hasty scribbled note
(Its source) would give away
The immortality
Your life's emotions claim?

To your notion, whatever the cause,
Belongs an essential truth:
Humankind's recognition
Of time outside human scale –
Even the deathbed blaze
Of once beneficent suns.

4

Why do we return? Not in the darkened rooms
Of rattling tambourines and butter muslin;
But as you boil an egg or make the bed
    You hear us and answer: 'Darling?'

Yes, that's our wish, after all, whatever ancient
Boredom or intervening cause of unwelcome
Would face us, for our presence once again
    To be taken all for granted.

We don't come in actuality, alas!
For we're in a place that even cosmologists,
Speculating on collapsed stars and anti-matter,
    Couldn't find more alien.

SAINTS AND STOICS

To P. H. Newby

Forced down the wild peninsula, the saints
Crossed to the island craved by no one else.
Beyond that, only Atlantis, paradise.
Pathetic the resting places on the way:
This mousy church, in size a mere waiting-room
(As earth for human life, so some assert) –
A native font; decaying mural daubs;
Thatched roof; three-letter date cut in the wall.
By the remains of the ash-grove, hop vines
And fruit trees that sustained the bygone fathers.
And round the churchyard, egg-shaped in the custom
Of long ago, the danesberry flourishes still,
Imagined by the one-track-minded troops
To have an aphrodisiac effect.
Mavises litter the horizontal tombs
With broken snail-shells. Under the altar rests
A seven-foot saint who may have named the church.

They say completion of the Parthenon
Left so many marble-carvers on the market
Even the country gods began to get
Marmoreal dedications. Quite unlike
The parsimonious art-work here. There are
Only three windows. Being illiterate
The congregations needed little light;
Two would have served, but lepers had a hole
Through which to see, as from cheap theatre places,
The Abbot raise the Blessed Sacrament.

Shrimps and their shadows on the contoured sand
Of the shallows: oddly, the shadows more apparent.
Today the tide had white-trimmed waves and so
The air to the arching sky seemed full of sound.
Late afternoon, the sea turned a bluer blue:
Orange-burned bathers, distant reds and yellows
Of parasols, and clouts for modesty,
Were clustered as by a water-colourist.

Appearance of the second crop of teeth:
The change from prettiness to embryo
Femme fatale. And the continual rise
Of capable, strong, industrious characters –
Sure to prolong the *patria*'s repute –
Detected first in beauteous or precocious
Children. Such things almost relied upon
To cheer up later years, when bodily ills
Of old seem benign compared with new arrivals,
So that one comes to yearn for them as for
Even unsatisfactory former loves.

Yes, then the world was ready to be saved
But somehow the opportunity was missed.
Grass grew up through the long straight street designed
To hold the border city. Since myself
Had gone back home from years of consular exile,
The letters from my stoic mentor ceased.
And time elapsed before the waves began
Of other, more barbarous, infidel invaders:
Yet somehow the opportunity was missed.

Sea winds at night still peal the ghostly bell.
Sleepless, I hear it, back on the frontiers of
The empire. But who else is there to hear;
The congregation shrivelled, lepers cured?
And somehow I've become as old as he
Who sent those epistles in former years and briefly
(It seems) preceded me in saying goodbye
To a strange world. Act of no significance:
For men of science the difference between
Past, present and future is a mere illusion,
Granted a stubborn one. My teacher wrote:
'The queer thing is, about our growing old,
We slowly lose our sense of being with
The here and now: one's as it were transposed
Into infinity, more or less alone,
No longer with hopes or fears, only observing.'
That's how I feel, though much less stoical!

Camomile on the dunes, astounding flowers –
Gold, white and tough as those recurring children.
And half sunk by sand, a hulk as sparely ribbed
As if the remains of one that brought the pirates.
An oar-winged wasp probed each of them in turn;
And peering in the rotten, sea-blanched timber
I made out the entrance to a nest – what dim,
Romantic, ingenious columns stretched beyond,
Home for the insect, gothic galleries!
The triumph of instinct there as ours is
The triumph – I was going to say 'of thought'
Then thought of what goes on in man below.

Answering questions in my seminars
Put by the most assiduous attenders
(Neurotics, provincial boys, unwashed old girls),
I say: 'Don't fret. Most humans contemplate
With terror the end of life. But that's a way
Of nature to conserve the species: rationally
The fear's unjustified. There's no more risk
Of disaster to the dead than to those unborn.'

Possibly swallows were nesting in the barn
Even in saints' times, feigning mere delight
In air, or aerial insect-gobbling, then
Swooping in at the broken door. Unlike the saints
They know from fate how vain it is to pray
For the coming of God's kingdom on this earth.

When, as it will, the empire shrinks and again
I'm ordered home, who will recall the days
When saints were giant, smelly, island men?

THE SLOTH MOTH

One of life's riddles solved, at least! The moth
That seems to spend its existence on the sloth
(Feeding perhaps on fur or sweat or spit)
Fell under suspicion when no trace of it
In either egg or larval form could be
Descried in the fur. From a sloth in captivity
Moths were removed, their eggs were hatched, and lo!
The larvae would not feed upon the slow
Animal's hide, nor even upon leaves from trees
That sloths inhabit. The only food to please
Was sloth dung. With that clue, biologists
Soon found (through half-obscuring brush and mists)
Among the pellets on the forest floor
Silk tubes that larvae spin! They, when mature,
Pupate in the dung pile, then the fresh-hatched moths
Fly up (to seek and settle on new sloths)
Towards the sun-coined forest canopy.
Thus it turns out the parasite must see
Its host as little more than one providing
Convenient dung and only riding, riding,
So as to be at hand when (sluggish in these
As all their motions) weekly the sloths descend the trees.

MUSICAL OFFERING

Composers and Executants

Required: some daring emendation to life,
A real 'I think thee Ariel';
And thorough heroism and cosiness,
As in Debussy's ballet 'the wounded soldier
Is tended by the affectionate doll.'

The thirty-eight works for girl bassoonists
Studying in the musical orphanage:
What dedication to female youth, and art!
Moreover, the carroty composer, in celibate orders,
Must be absolved from ambiguous intent.

Actual smiles at Mimi's coughs and sobbing –
For the consummate reprise they punctuate –
Shakings benign of heads, as though the composer
Were not with Edward VII or the dead Infanta
But knew how the years approved his slowish tunes.

The western sky is pale as a complexion;
Passes like drying blood from red to dark.
Under the planets, long-legged spiders sleep
Close to earth. All species aspire to comfort –
'The wedding will be fun. Bears are good dancers.'

Evenings of playing Schumann rather badly
Must yield, as time moves on, to worse affairs –
The sparkling girlish mane next to a madman;
From filial love and intellectual accord
Depart the proud Oistrakh and Shostakovitch fathers.

Broadcast Concert

The Strauss last songs. The solo violin,
Perhaps through too much feeling, makes a boner.
Forgiven! Tears merely run
For human frailty the sooner.

Granados: Escenas Poeticas *and* Libro de Horas

Third-rate, one thinks, but truly meditative:
Perhaps as poets' Muzak it may live.

And then some harrowing melody comes out
Of the turning disc and half removes the doubt.

Besides, since youth, age or bizarre disaster
Tends somehow to confirm the rank of master,

Behind the notes one hears 1916 –
The fatal tin-fish from the Boche submarine.

Quartets

'A willow or acacia over my brother's grave'
– Beethoven's epigraph for that *adagio*
Ceases to shock or puzzle (his brothers then alive!)
      As soon as we come to know

His elder brother had expired in infancy,
Relinquishing the name of Ludwig. Shakespearean
(As might have been prognosticated), the family
      Bed-life that formed the man.

Like all our worlds, mysterious but commonplace
Geniuses' worlds: how else could mortals contemplate
Quartets whose prolongations are designed to face
      With thanks the fangs of fate?

What different pain, nocturnal memories of things
Limping about the house we failed to see or bless,
From the great grief of varying keys and time that brings
      Mercy and happiness!

Opera

A sky, a westering August sun. But all at once
I realise the season of avian opera's over;
So not so perfect as I thought, this ambience
Of warmth, of dusk and colour – lasting, it seemed, for ever.

Musical History

Need Mahler's melodramatic protestation
Have been succeeded by the twelve-tone scale?
Mahler could well have been an aberration;
Schoenberg a later Brahms – or small-town nut.
Would then some saner, blither song have cut
Two wars and Jewry's woe out of life's tale?

Satie's Jack in the Box

The score turned up quite grizzled with neglect.
He thought he'd left it on an omnibus,
And died. But when they shifted his effects
The score turned up, quite grizzled with neglect,
Back of the antediluvian, erect
Piano. Though alive he'd made no fuss,
The score turned up. Quite grizzled with neglect,
He thought he'd left it on an omnibus.

Concerto

Will my great-grandchildren play
The first Max Bruch?
I mean, in that shrouded day
Will tunes still uncannily hook
The cynical clay?

Ricercar

'A fine sensibility to Music: does
Himself, with thrilling *adagios* on the flute,
Join in these harmonious acts' – and that's about
The only allusion to the Emperor's art
In the whole octave of volumes: even here
We may suspect was meant *'arpeggios'*!
Most pages body out the maps of men
In blocks, by streams, woods, soaking Europe's plains.

A wonder there isn't somewhere the anecdote
That Frederick's love of music failed to survive
Edentulousness and so the power to play –
His passion proving merely self-regard.
Quite absent from the index either Bach;
Also (it follows) the theme *recht Königlich*
Which to unwarlike persons such as I
Is Frederick's claim upon posterity.

Frederick the Great's long-winded pregnancy
Made Jane's valetudinarianism grow
More founded. Finally, the brougham's driver
Saw as they bowled along near Stanhope Gate
The still, tiered hands were dead. The widower
Recalled her overseeing the making of
A writing-room more apt for *Frederick*'s girth:
The attic at Cheyne Row – continental climate!

A rotten architect and 'Irish hodmen',
Bad workmanship ('mendacity of hand'),
Bloomers like Arnott's Grate, self-styled 'Improved',
Made the whole project one more in the line
Of the Carlyles' unprussianlike campaigns
Against such foes as hens, for allies like sleep.
O 'Demon-Fowls' next door; night vigils; heartburn:
Ongoing years of all neurotic souls!

Remembrance after the once-beloved's death
Inspires a new, a tear-inducing style:
Conjugal love, notoriously awkward
Ever to paint with verisimilitude.
Rational art is equally half-willed –
Canons' sequential volleys in the mind:
Acrostics: 'Gentlemen, old Bach is here.'
Rising of tough musicians, no doubt, in homage.

HEDGE-SPARROWS AND HOUSE-SPARROWS

Our medieval fathers simply named
All small birds sparrows. Hence the absurdity
Of calling these March strangers to the garden
Hedge-sparrows. Bills not the pyramids required
For seed-cracking, chassis altogether longer,
More Italianate, and striped along the back,
This couple trill as constantly as late
Beethoven, restless in trees, and skimming to the border.

I read, you nest in April. Stay till then
And populate our homely area
With dashing aviators, tireless songsters.
But how will you survive the silent hedge-cats
Consoling, too, mankind's suburban life;
Find nourishment, in face of chemical
Warfare against our little green invaders?
I hope my welcome's not as treacherous as Cawdor's.

No wonder that the name's a term of endearment –
'Let me but kiss your eyes, my sweet, my sparrow.'
Even the man-sized ostrich some will know
As the sparrow-camel. Sparrowcide denotes
Destruction of sparrows. Preserve us from that crime.
Instead, let there be sparrowdom, the reign
Of sparrows, for sustaining your kin in name
At least suggests some worth in human habitations.

ON HIS SIXTIETH BIRTHDAY

Fathers must tell their children of injustice
And cruelty, between the rewarding toil
Of lessons on the bassethorn and readings
Aloud of Arthur Conan Doyle.

Some of life's sense, I think, if sense at all,
Resides in the minor artist's artifact:
The variations on a small perception
Heroically destined for neglect;

That anguished harmony, those chiming stanzas,
Whiskers and twigs set down painstakingly –
Left for improbable future recognition
Like girls grown up from storm-launched infancy.

Curious that the robin was observed
By villein, monarch, merchant, factory-hand.
But if I look behind me to the fork,
Oblique in the garden, my particular friend

(Warily glancing back on straddled pins)
Has extra white along his foggy wings.
There are as many different birds as poets;
One bird despite man's botched imaginings.

Wrong, wrong to say that February's mild,
Equally that the Sabine month's severe.
In age we come to welcome February
For what he is, of arbitrary power.

The stares' preliminary coughing: will
Fate let me see them through to actual lieder?
Already I'm consoled by tiny green
Arches that gothicize the frosty border.

Yet, glimpsed below disordered grasses, man's
All-muddled footfalls printed in the mud
Remind us awesomely that still to come
Is the atrocious murder of the god.

So often art's devices are naive:
The watchman's horn after the fugal flurry
Sounding again, a true goodnight; the axe
Struck in the flies on anything but cherry –

Paralleled by the care of man for men:
Such private trouble as is taken by
Schoolmaster referees and wholesome nurses –
The other love that makes us want to cry.

Now oceanographers believe that oceans
Are transient, that even Asias move
Around, like sandwiches, on rocky salvers.
Thus the blue swelling of the globe may prove

To mask calamities far worse than they
Create. Small wonder then that life's a mess,
Its very scenery not yet arranged
To satisfy the director's finickiness.

And can the state of art surprise us when
We contemplate the diathesis of the State –
Though half expecting artists' very weakness
Will somehow make mankind inviolate?

So, sneezing in this cold, bare kingdom, one
Dreams wildly: yes, I may be there for Spring –
Meaning, say, for the end of tyranny,
Meaning the start of some great profluent thing.

And almost one feels sorry, finally,
For February, its lugubrious
Austerity so threatened by renewal.
Threatened, one says, but knowing that the tree

Can't help the shuddering rising of the sap,
Descent of blushing tassels, sparkling stars –
That even now one's faith makes out in those
Nailed branches black against the sunset's bars.

DREAMLESS NIGHT

To Anthony Thwaite

Long night of dreamless sleep!
The problem's how to enjoy it,
Since there's no wakening –
And perhaps no premonition
Of that untypical
Turn to a conscientious
Life of insomnia.

Essential to say farewell
To unsleeping's very pleasures;
And to guarantee the gifts
Of a sanguine testament –
Puzzling strategy for
A being so thoroughly
Secular and not top-notch.

Why days must end in sleep –
The natural contraption –
Is what's in question here:
Uneasy resting-place
In the botheration between
One's fundamental states
Of molecular endurance.

The status of a world
Of deep ties and fascination
Made by mere butterflies,
Itself an eternal sliver,
Falls for evaluation
Also, but surely not
By its partial citizen.

On August's setting sun
The air is seen to be full
Of tiny creatures: so
Who says there won't at night,
In the dark above our bed,
Be wings, the unsuspected
Guardians of quitted dreams?

Some liken the process to
A voyage, the traveller only
Slowly aware of his port.
Rather, one's packaged under
Hatches and scarcely conscious
Even of the throb of going,
The susurration of seas.

Is it all voyaging then?
I suppose we'd hope at last
To land on a marvellous
But ill-governed coast, as before;
And try with our weak equipment
Its order to amend,
Leave it with words to ponder.

VISITING THE GREAT

One hears of visitors finding a caramel
Adhering to their pants after visiting
The great man, or a tale about his farting
In unreceptive company, or less
Dramatic turns of art or statesmanship
    In the realms of the all-too-human.

Those even of the slightest fame to prompt
Strangers to call will scarcely be surprised.
Our wonder is the chronic expectation
That flawless marble, perfect tailoring,
And flow of wisdom should be available
    Some dozy afternoon.

The elevation of the treaty or
Sonnet above our everyday concerns
Always gives ground for marvel or suspicion –
The authors, unless quite grossly self-deluding,
Only too conscious of the secret clause
    Blurred with their tears or snot.

Yet something in the famous corresponds
To the devoutness of the hoi polloi.
The small-talk of the gods, their dirty deeds
With wine-waiters or river nymphs, detract
Not at all from moments when the thunder barks
    And flora shifts its roots.

While being catechised, the subject broods
On matters that preoccupy his hours:
How could men weld the special instruments
Designed to scald the feet or crack the skull;
Arrange in advance, like dining-rooms, the neat
    Areas of torture.

Gloomily thinking: yet it still goes on –
Craftsmen replaced by great production lines.
What is the human? Difficult to say.
Back in a place of more mundane endeavour,
The hairy sweetmeat is detached and pondered
    But no conclusion reached.

CINQUAINS

April.
The chestnut lifts
White tapered hands from which
Have naturally fallen back
Green cuffs

Sparrow!
I see why you
Find the invisible:
Your eyes are suitably so near
The floor.

Glitter
Of leaves in clear
And steady moonlight means
No more than that they just were rinsed
By rain.

Midnight.
A moidered mind –
Yet sensing all that may
Go wrong in what it must drag out
Of bed.

I have
To pause and think:
Did she live long enough,
My mother, to know my grandchild's
Mother?

Shaving,
I see between
My lower teeth spaces
Typical of the jaw of some
Old skull.

After
The washing-up,
Two objects by the sink,
Left perhaps by Ancient Britons:
Blue hands.

NO MILK –
The message blurs
As days go by and rain
Falls in the lane upon the blown
Paper.

Sequel
To death: a life's
Collection of pictures
Sold by one's executors for
Peanuts.

You tell
A brief, chill tale
Of childless friends of old:
You know they had a baby-girl
That died?

Spiders,
With all their legs,
Over irregular
Terrain step lightly as well-bred
Horses.

Bright eyes
Of otters, seen
In some TV programme;
Of female blackbirds in April;
And girls.

Humans
Each possessing
Eyes *sui generis* –
Unlike these brown-beaded begging
Sparrows.

Gentle,
Sad – gorillas.
So observation proves.
As Rochester turned out as soft
As Jane.

Blossom
In May, scattered
As profusely as snow;
Lilac indoors smelling nearly
Rotten.

Touch-down.
But only quite
Long after does the world
Of sound with suddenness remove
Its mute.

Planting
Hyacinths, I
Think: I'll see them again –
So many poets dead this year,
I'm safe.

Strange bird,
You follow me
Round the garden, calling
Most when I pause ... My secateurs'
Squeaking!

A thrush –
Even before
The end of the old year –
On the bare damson tree, fluting
In rain.

Bonfires.
White smoke pouring
Through the unsunlit air;
Leaving grey craters in the piles
Of bronze.

It is –
It has to be –
The living who provide
Comfort for the dying, such as
It is.

SCHOOL TIME, WORK TIME

From the car's back seat he looks on
Legs long enough for a swan's dance;
Perhaps white-stockinged, like horses'.
Any such young girls, by wild chance
Glancing inside, see papers spread
Apropos some cool million.
Grave nonsense of bonds and bourses:
Glass case of the mummified dead.

OXFORD ALBUM

My footfalls faintly sag the eroded stair.
Through a strait gate the garden of the Fellows.
The awesome line of tenants of the Chair.
March's male sparrows black-faced as Othellos.

The coloured scutcheons of the founding earls
Dim libraries of brown or golden hair.
The dreams of dons are dwarfs and little girls.
My breath augments the whited valley air.

Should time condemn the passionate to be
Oblates of culture in culture's disrepair,
Here will they raise the mocking effigy
Of emperors who deployed the ironware.

If lions may be said to live in yellows
That hue pervades the fenestrated twirls.
Youth pulses through the strangled artery
And knowledge tries to fascinate the fair.

NOTEBOOK

A seven-spotted ladybird
Toddles across the sheet
To which I feel I can't add a word.
Then opening like some cute
Trinket by Fabergé,
It flies with angelic suddenness away.

The book seems dead with things
I've left behind. I want
As ever to start again – on wings
Instead of feet. Yet aren't
To this new world the keys
Pedestrian particularities?

TWO BLOND FLAUTISTS

Bath-water still and tinted as lagoons;
Animal Farm turned back behind the taps;
Shampoo uncapped; all towels on the floor –
The child's abandoned these for rather more
Fruitful and interesting turns of life.
I fondly sigh and dive to shift the plug;
Tidy up book and bottle; make the fold
Follow the stripe, as favoured by the old.
I'm not the last who's going to be her mug,
I think, as Poulenc rises from beneath,
Temperate and punctual as her propelling breath.

A goldcrest probes the wall time has de-mortared.
So rare a creature in the suburbs! I
Daren't stir till its acrobatics end – at first
Puzzled to name a blond streak on a midget.
Later, as stuttery as a flute, the fidget
Sings self-betrayingly. How blest are those
Destiny has engardened and grand-daughtered!
How forceful the flitting shape, green-toned like flesh
Yet actually brown! They merely prove,
The growing days, the truism that all life,
The frailest even, *ipso facto* means to live.

140 YEARS ON

Green leaves with deepening edge of fawn,
   With web of brilliants panoplied,
     And as upon a coffin lid
The thud of apples on the lawn.

That of his own estate he's lord
   Is bruited by the robin's song:
     Now the domain of human wrong
He comes to cock an eye toward.

I take my book beyond the shade
   And open it and read those great
     Lines measured with the rule of eight;
The roman titles time has made

Seem less inscrutable; and see,
   As though the tears were still undried,
     A note that Arthur Hallam died
This day in 1833.

Friendship divorced from flesh – how right
   And precious in our youth! And yet
   If age regrets, it will regret
Loss of youth's other appetite.

Seasons revolve; thought on its stair
   Toils up, and so men deem it odd
   That once geology and God
Combined to bring them to despair.

What point in nature having been
   So careful of the species, should
   Her highest instrument for good
(As a coarse gardener's thumb wipes clean

The aphis from a budded rose)
   Cancel the living from the sphere,
   Pursuing the insane idea
That creatures like themselves are foes?

Blood starting from the creeper nailed
   On the crossed wood somehow confirms
   It's not the derms and ectoderms
But man's response to myth that's failed.

Evening: the robin silent; trees
   Dark on a cloudless, still-bright sky –
   The near trees calm, but modestly
The far stirred by a transient breeze.

The scene so beautiful perhaps
   Because unhaltable the hour –
   As though the extent of summer's power
Were reckoned by the day's collapse.

Comes home to me Vienna's fate
   After that time-bomb vessel near
   The brain burst in the former clear
And sanguine days of bourgeois state –

Fate the more bleak through history's blur,
   Seen from an epoch still ill-tuned:
   He who dressed our unhealing wound,
Ex-doctor of the Berggasse;

Or the triumphal entry of
   The maniac's blond automata ...
   We lucky old, who seem so far
Beyond the worst of war and love,

What ships may yet sail in our heart
   With those who died outside our care,
   And lodge their cargoes ice-bound there,
Through winters of solitary art!

ON BIRKETT MARSHALL'S

RARE POEMS OF THE SEVENTEENTH CENTURY

Coppinger, Pordage, Collop, Fayne,
Fettiplace, Farley, Chamberlain –

They could be the darling poets of my youth:
I almost search among the names for mine.

All have remunerative occupations –
Physician, milliner, playwright, baronet!

Some are locked in a single year – 'alive'
In '62 or 'floruit' '39.

Nothing is known of Pick or Prestwich. Still,
Small wonder what's behind the poetry fades.

Three hundred years ago they were consoled
For lack of genius and fame by some

Astonishing trope or stanza's tailoring.
Strange that the consolation still should work

– Prujean, 'Ephelia', Cutts, Cockayne,
Cameron, Allott, Fuller, Raine.

1935–75

The toothless men of Sind; a faceless lamb;
Hairless mutations in the Norway rat;
The Ishmaels and the Roosevelts; the big
Robertson strain of the Washington navel orange;
Three kinds of triplets; silver guinea-pigs;
The giant salivary chromosomes;
A year of sterilization in Germany;
And polydactyly in swine, in humans –
Having conveyed it home, I wonder how
I could initially have baulked (through sheer
Meanness) at buying from the outside stall
The gathered issues of *The Journal of
Heredity* for 1935.

For all seems poetry – and largely in
Blank verse! – and pregnant with the innocence
(As of great tribal bards) of scientists.

And all put forth when I was twenty-two
And twenty-three. The binding's been in some
Storm – more than showers on the fivepence box;
Say, hoses playing over fires begun
By sterilizing Germans, who in fact
Were helped appropriately from the eugenics scene
By one of the 'superior' Roosevelts.

This summer of '75 I bedded out
Blossoms striped red and white like footballers,
The end result of doings reported here,
No doubt: that is, the x-irradiation
Of relatively plain petunia stocks.

What Faustian knowledge that in youth could daunt
Beyond my previous ideas of doom!
We saw the photographs of buttocks beaten
Perhaps by six-fingered hands; great oranges
Left to decay remote from hungry lands:
Yet watching Madame Butterfly look over
La rada, il porto, la città di Nagasaki,
Our tears were still for dirty tricks done to
A single member of the nation-state.

AUTUMNAL METAMORPHOSES

A rather untidy bird soars up – a leaf!
Southward, a slanting light from pie-crust cloud.
Trees ginger as a cat. Long shadows cast
At noon. Your breath condenses or will soon
Condense on your moustache. The creeper's changed
Into a red disease of walls. To catch
The post that goes at seven you skim through near
Dark, sanguine flies, invisible filaments.

In houses chequered with yellow windows children
Already hear that gormless sons of kings
Do better than their cunning brothers; that
Small toads turn to lovely girls if put inside
Hollowed-out carrots. Soon, whole families
Will dream of their extraordinary desires.

CRISIS

O courteous ladies of the West Countree!
Visiting Plymouth for the BBC,
I saw in Debenham & Freebody

'Trousers reduced'. And marched into the store –
Trousers sardined in stands upon the floor,
Trousers that won the West, that Oxford wore.

Wanting a pair to work in in the garden,
Before inflating prices further harden,
I laughingly begged the shop assistant's pardon

And asked her if among the azure jeans –
Although a style intended for the teens
Or certainly especially for the lean –

Something might fit one rather broadly-based,
An ageing man, a man without much waist.
'I'm sure there is,' she said, quite poker-faced.

And added: 'Do you know his measurements?'
Dear lady, how experienced with gents!
I meant myself. You twigged. And so I went

Smugly across the Hoe to my hotel,
Pants in a carrier. Against the hell
Of sunset the statue of the admiral

Looked out to Cadiz or the Spanish Main.
On seas courageous and in shops urbane,
Surely our England must be great again.

THE OLD TOY

Bits of me keep falling off;
bits don't work properly;
and other bits are broken
by the girl who owns me.

O vanishing teeth that crunch
things I still love; O part
I know can't now be mended;
O miniature heart!

IN HIS SIXTY-FIFTH YEAR

The October of His Sixty-fifth Year

With beak about as long and hinged as chopsticks,
The starling stabbing among the chocolate whorls
Is speckled like a specimen of quartz,
Except the slanted settings for the eyes
Which are as dark as those of belly-dancers.

Strange that obsessive observation seems
To be an overture to verse – as strange
As wriggling food preceding avian art.

Should old age act as though its missing teeth
And fading sight were mere stage properties
Irrelevant to its response to life –
Which ought to be as though demise were still
As lightly contemplated as in youth?

Ideal arrangement; rarely met, however –
Like that prescription of the Danish sage:
'It's a good thing for monarchs to be ugly.'

Bird-brains somewhat exaggeratedly
Counter the seasons' revolutions: man's
Presumably perturb them not at all.

Not for them huge errors of intelligence
Like Sorel's, who before the First World War
Tried to enoble violence, which he thought
Was on the downgrade – to the detriment
Of efficacious social struggle – though
In fact a Time of Troubles loomed. Still here!

Maniacs salute annihilating missiles,
And English-beetle nourished nightingales
Winter among the zebras of Zaire.

Getting His Daimler Out at Night

In 1912 Rachmaninov complained
About his motor's poor acceleration . . .
Just such a desultory joky start
I'd deprecate in other poets' art.

Beyond the dark garden, garaged, is my own –
Almost, it seems, as ancient as Sergei
Vasilyevich's – waiting doggedly,
Like some old patient on the National Health,

For rare spares that will staunch her bleeding gears.
The scuffed blue leather hugs my funny-bone;
Her ton and a half through nearly fourteen years
Has been a purring, savage part of me.

I wonder if I'll scrap the rusting monster
Before I die and buy an automobile
More suited to my later modest style.
Who cares? How right Karl Popper was to say:

'What makes a work of art significant
Is something quite different from self-expression.'
I can't take in the early winter sky,
Seen as I go to unstable those yoked mares:

Too much of it, too complex, too bizarre.
Besides, one's mind is fixed on earthly things;
Flesh shivering. The artist still concerned
About the acceleration of his car!

'It's hard to write a melody,' announced
A critic in *The Times* in other day:
Rather belated witness in our age.
The engine of Rachmaninov, for long

Imagined by others, too, to be a crock
Still eats the years, not far behind the leaders.
Is it the Way, that milky arch of lace,
My dim eyes (born in 1912) enquire;

Or a still cloud against the gulfs of space?

Childhood In the Early Twentieth Century

Even in careless hours
Death's served up with our life:
The memory of friends
Now dead, and of their ends.
– Except in our infancy,
I was about to qualify,
Then thought of former days
When early death was rife.
– Days of my own, indeed.
So did I never play
In perfect happiness,
But set out my regiments
Knowing their bloody fate;
And kissed my widowed mother,
Teased my surviving brother,
Scared of some ghastly face
Upstairs, on sheets of joy?

1976 Draws To a Close

Youth happens only once. I mean, my dreams
Were of us kissing; but being sixty-four –
The age I really am – she as she was
When first we met and fell in love – the world,
I knew, would be censorious to see
A young girl wasted in an old man's arms.

They seek a mate for George and if in vain
He well may be the last one of his kind –
Sub-species of the weird Galapagos
Tortoise, already sixty years of age.
(Though reading on I'm reassured to find
He's likely to clock up a hundred more.)

In the same issue of *The Times* I see
That dead at eighty-five, in Munich, on
Tuesday, November thirtieth, is Rasp –
Sinister villain of the cinema
Of Lang. I guess it was 1931
In a flea-pit that still clung to silent films,

On the back row, I watched *Die Frau im Mond*
And through her hair Fritz Rasp, abrasive as
His name. The passion of specific years –
Never repeated – unrepeatable . . .
Yet strangely I class myself with George, as did
No doubt old Rasp, in Germany, last week.

December 2, 1976

Who knows or, if they knew, would care
That Phyllis Monkman, dead today
At eighty-four, a 'dancer and light
Comedienne', was a favourite
Of my mother's and, sedate yet gay,
The name beguiled my infant ear?

Probably even then my love
Of withers-wringing tunes was there,
For don't I still a chorus croak
From my first concept of a work
Of art: that show *Bing Boys Are Here?*
– Where 'the idol of the troops on leave'

Réchauffé what the Somme had chilled.
I do a sum and with surprise
See she was four years younger than
My mother – who might still have been
The survivor. Strange, in such a case
To have found ourselves today both old.

Singing, 1977

For most of my life, no need to wear specs.
Now I look over them at meetings
With the aplomb of a rotten actor,
Push them around my bumf when spouting,
Needlessly checking the earpieces' hinges.
Of all my portraits I say: poor likeness.
'Colonel (Retired)' or 'Disgusted' stares out,
Doomed to expire of apoplexy;
Whitening moustache, jaw-line sagging.
Like a woman, I think: I've lost my looks.
Reactionary views, advanced mostly
To raise a laugh – taken as gospel!

I've bought these discs of piano music
By Granados – largely unexplored;
And if asked who I'd take to a desert island,
Him or who'd be just as novel, Schoenberg,
Who doubts an elderly buffer would choose
The melodious Debussyan Spaniard?

As a matter of fact I'd not mind taking
The words and music of Johnny Mercer,
Even discounting what really biffs me –
That after the euphemistic 'long illness'
He died in a year of his seventh decade
(Strange years, and each year seeming more strange),
The departed gold summer of '76.
Only the weather will return in the vintage,
Perhaps a corked bottle or two recalling
How bitter some days were to swallow,
Prompting thanks for more commonplace years.

Mercer's pushing the case, of course;
As we do in Cheltenham or Tunbridge Wells.

My life's been a story of ignorance.
I never even used to know
How spiders adhered to walls in winter
(Like blots that need blowing up to be decoded),
Challenging man to accept hibernation;
That wind keeps old folk, like babies, wakeful.
No record made: passion undeclared.

At the junketings for my son's sixty-fifth
I'll be pinching his thunder by nearing
My ninetieth. Not that he'll mind.
Jerome Kern's 'They'll never believe me'
(Pre-dating the torpedoing of Granados!)
And that mysterious Mercer line,
As though from an Edwardian operetta:
'There's a dance pavilion in the rain' –
Things I so often sing, by then
Mad time will have made even quainter.

But could I possibly still own a voice?
Curious enough at sixty-five –
A blessing, too; that sons may note at forty –
Even though one messes about perversely,
Trying, say, four-beat unrhymed lines
Which no decent poet, except Arthur Waley,
Has ever managed to get off the ground.

And why so ego-centred the content?
Emblematic, I try to persuade myself,
Of the entire human condition –
Composers who die in usual pain,
Who drown, meaning to rescue their wives,
Regular soldiers, rain-moulded dancers,
Work of joy and disappointment,
Life of creativeness and bereavement . . .

Peering at some enigmatic blot,
Groping for my glasses in the night-time.

VOLUMINOUS ART, SHORT LIFE

Wordsworth's poems arrive, in chronological order;
Hardy and Auden entire already on the table.
Friends and strange poetasters send me volumes much
Slimmer but somehow taking equally long to read.

I've decided at last to look into Hartley Coleridge;
And perhaps expose the myth that Hopkins's poetry
Had something to do with speech. What time for murder
   stories?
Even in the early nineteenth century (or so

I glean from Thomas Moore's journal) *Paradise Regained*
Was seen to have more supernumerary syllables
Than its predecessor. Should I check this allegation?
A great sense of the potty, Moore: must *his* verse be ploughed
   through?

As is my habit I stick up on the kitchen wall
The cutting from *The Times* about the mensual sky.
It seems only yesterday that Venus was too near the sun
To be seen; and now she's showy in the early night.

Thus July merges into February for the old.
I glance with most curiosity at the end of Wordsworth.
Lord Lyttleton, kicked downstairs for calling Lady Archer
A drunken peacock on account of her dress and rainbow
   feathers,

Had also rolled a piece of blancmange into a ball
And covering it with 'variegated comfits' pronounced:
'This is the sort of egg a drunken peacock would lay.'
But not long from Tom Moore's youth to Daddy
   Wordsworth's decay.

SHOP TALK

'We have the mauve or the cerise,
And of course the peach.'

'I think that striped is gorgeous.'

'Can these be repaired again?'
'I'm afraid it's your welt that's gone.'

'Four packets of Player's, please.'
'These ones?' 'Those ones.'

'Have you got the *I, Claudius*?'

'Is it real cream in them buns?'

Poor voices, calling each to each,
In a strange but transparent idiom
(So I think, the ageing bard, all-knowing).

'Hi, dad, you're forgetting your stamps!' So I am.
Another world is also going.

QUATRAINS OF AN ELDERLY MAN

Summer's End

A wasp starts burrowing in my naked toe,
No doubt preparatory to laying eggs.
Does it imagine I'm already dead
Or is it one that dooms a living host?

In the Night

I wake up, vaguely terrified, at three
And switch the light on, reach out for my book,
And slip inside the life of sanity
Of Wopsle, Gargery and Pumblechook.

South-East London

I witnessed the disappearance of the tram,
The trolley-buses' rise and fall, but who'd
Have thought to see a change of climate come –
Hefty black schoolgirls in the Old Kent Road?

Low Tide at Greenwich

BEWARE OF CRANES (it says) but all I see
Are swans at the river's edge, past rusty wrecks
Of piles and barges, preening on polished mud
Their dazzling hulls with dislocated necks.

Listening

I still can tell from high fidelity,
Thank God, low ditto: yet who cares how thin,
When certain cadences get under way,
The fossil baritone or violin?

Writing

What verses, even now, I judge I write!
– Almost as decent as I hope they'll be.
These are the verses I compose at night
When booze suspends my judging faculty.

Poetry and Whist

How enviable Herrick's
Fourteen hundred lyrics!
– Though, as the Scot complained when they dealt him all
The trumps, a lot of them were small.

Robbed

Somewhere along the way I changed my person
With an old man. Where is he now, that thief?
Perhaps enjoying in my flesh exertion
Only a criminal could carry off.

Late-born Infants

His last few cycles for piano Brahms
Described as lullabies of his own sadness.
What marvellous things old men hold in their arms,
That sleep and wake and bring them fleeting gladness!

The Metaphysical

Donne took his propositions much as tricks
To induce belief in something really true.
Strange world, where legs are merely two straight sticks,
Yet flesh turns into spirit at their screw.

Dreams

It's dreams of jealousy that now give pain,
Not jealousy itself. The feeling's gone
In actual life – as well as the beauteous, vain
Possession it spied and grew viridian on.

Time

It seems, because of inactivity,
That sombre suits, black shoes and motor-cars
Last longer. But meantime across my eye
Flickers the yearly shifting of the stars.

Ordinary Seaman

> The 143ft mast of *HMS Ganges* at Shotley, Suffolk, has been listed as a monument by the Department of the Environment – news item, 1976

Inscribe thereon that in 1941
I climbed it twice in fright.
Once as routine but also (to make sure
I dared) the previous night.

Winter

I step from the house at nightfall, thereby knowing
How startlingly life continues in the wild –
Far traffic's pedal, trees very quietly growing,
The air as cool as kisses of a child.

Pacifism

Utterly strange babies offer sucks of lollies,
Like ants to aggressor ants: propitiation
Needless for me. But what more venal follies
Will they commit when *they* form the invasion?

High Up

Pruning an apple-tree among the birds –
Each keeping nonetheless its self-judged distance –
I marvel at the spate of avian words
Through January's still unthawed resistance.

January 1977

New Moon near Venus on the twenty-third,
The satellite's rondure underlined in fire;
Its face ambiguous in the brownish shade:
Love's tiny planet blurred as through a tear.

Kissing on the Bus

Surely I'd be as concerned about other lives
As about my own had I the entrée to them.
As it is, I sneer at these public youthful loves
And smugly read the obituary column.

Accident

My briefcase falls open in the street. Displayed:
Aspirins for migraine, chocolates for my wife.
Despite my 'Oh, bugger', strangers come to aid
The old boy picking up his bits of life.

Winter's End

Match-heads of white and ochre on the jade
Match-sticks of snowdrop and crocus; almost pink
Warty excrescences on the peach's twig:
And suddenly birds have time to sing and chase.

Laziness

In the June garden, as supine I lie,
An aircraft's great white loosening cable of exhaust
Blows over. Then the flawless heavens defy
The finding of emblems for a future holocaust.

ON HIS SIXTY-FIFTH BIRTHDAY

Went to the Mini-Town Hall
(So-called) to claim my free
Pass for the off-peak bus.
No one expressed surprise
That I was sixty-five –
Stunned at my sprightly gait
And thick if frosted hair.
The ladies around were concerned
With reduced-price Ovaltine
And other baksheesh of the State,
Befitting their unamorous age.

The tawdry building was set
In bogland off the A2:
Blown paper white as the gulls
On the stud-dented fields of play
Deserted now in the sun-
Shot end of a winter day
By home-wending girls and boys.

O feet-distorting shoes,
Lung-changing cigarettes,
How necessary to youth
And painful to contemplate
For the busy-bodying old!
With desperation – or so
Sometimes it seems to me –
I hang on to what they waste
As once I wasted it.

Somewhere I read – what confirms
My sentient life of late –
'Old men cry easily.'
Who would have thought I should mourn
The future of healthy louts,
The bunions of pretty girls?
The heavens sufficiently ope
To show the worn gold ring
Of the moon's beginning light.
Such mild observations fall
In the 'pindarics' used
By Arnold for his laments
Over his father, dead;
Wordsworth; the Kraut who took
So long to die in France;
And the multiple Brontës, dead.

For arraigning England he forgave
Heine – since 'we echo her foes'.
How much easier to forgive
Would Arnold find it today
When our 'glory, genius and joy'
Are sunk to a still lower notch!

The sparrow – commonplace, small:
Yes, that is confirmed when a bird
Hops strangely into the house.
And I cup it in my hands
To counter what chilling shock
Brought it to seek the help
Of those impuissant enough
In tragedies of their own.
But beautiful also the bird:
The eye a tiny gem
Found in a bundle of rags.
How quickly one gets to know
A fellow creature – the marks
That make each one unique
(Including such accidents
As a beak with adhering bread)
And even hidden traits
That the character underpin.

Next morning (as one had guessed)
He is dead, and I take him up –
Weightless, unwarm – to inter
Him where daffodils all look south.

Moss on the paving, furred
Like caterpillars, gold on green,
May be removed with Jeyes
Fluid, the wiseacres say.
Another way is to run
A Dutch hoe along the cracks –
Labour of many days,
Dead weight of material, doomed
To the socialist compost heap.

What other sproutings, more
Seemly to bourgeois souls,
These winter killings succeed –
Lilies of brown-moled white
Throats and the velvet rose!

Winter one day, the next
Balmily Spring, I throw
The artificial green
Of the first mowings upon
The oddly neutral pile.

Arnold would not have thought
The answer to England's ills,
Whatever it was, to be cold
Verse or hot Ovaltine.
Charm is what makes, he said,
The work of poets divine.
I well can understand
He would think these lines devoid
Of charm, stuck as they are
With the cares of a Philistine world.
Yet no one is more aware
Than I of the Beast-ruled age –
So might be thought lucky to hold
A 'Travel Permit For
Elderly Person' which must
In the end see one safely across
That dark and bitter stream
Beyond encircling hands
– Though in fact I would give it up
For another painful stay,
Cigarettes, corns and all,
On the parlous nearer shore.

BUCKLAND'S *CURIOSITIES OF NATURAL HISTORY*

A pallid worm drummed up by thunder-rain
In Spring's mere shin-high border
Still writhes like an insomniac although
I sprinkle it with soil;
No easier underground
Than in the rowdy, zig-zagged, yellow air.
Perhaps some bitter season of the soul
Has pitched it against the earth;
But no doubt what will conquer Conqueror Worm.

'Common shrimps are capital skeleton makers,'
Wrote Major Buckland, late
Assistant surgeon in the 2nd Life Guards.
Yes, fish (like birds) are always famished; worms
Also. Or so one might have thought before
Dealing with this neurotic specimen –
Its role changed as was Buckland's in a long
Pacific age when, freed from patching up
His fighting men, he met the Chinese giant
And measured Colonel Ramsay's giant tiger.

As to the race of tigers, the Major said,
Warmly, those preying on the human species
Were 'generally mangy and out of condition.'
Would he have argued that this worm's malaise
Might rise through making buried dry ribs dry?

The rain drives me in at last –
To Poulenc's setting of the strange motet
(For being simple somehow all the stranger)
Telling of that mysterious design
Whereby the animals
See God born in a manger –
Not only horizontally-chewing beasts
But also worms, like serpents charmed from baskets;
And tigers, hiding white saliva'd fangs
With black lips, sheathing their future bourgeois brooches
And even vowing (though
Who'd really trust long puss?)
To be for ever non-carnivorous . . .

Among the moist-eyed kings renouncing war.

MORNING

Through half-drawn curtains distant roses' daub
And a young blackbird, sepia still his prow,
Taking the berries of a berberis,
Each a pythagorean proposition
            Of angle, orb and tangents.

The iteration of the seasons must
Bring to me worsening health and history –
Such thoughts I waken to when noises hidden
In daytime wail far off or overhead
            Creak like John Gabriel Borkman.

And yet how raw one stays. I've never heard
Pronounced the word 'raceme' and look it up.
So much I've never read or heard. Perhaps
Some Spring within my reach will flower my long
            Unflowering wistaria.

As animals stagger up, amelioration
Of human ailments leads to ready tears
Of feeling for art and for the lives of others
And to activity in the noddle one thought
           Had ossified for ever.

This early Summer morning the aperture
Beneath the oriented bedroom door –
And even its keyhole – are incandescent with
The sun in the still somewhat shady room of nights,
           Thrilling as light in childhood.

What a startling notion, really against the whole
Philosophy of what I've always thought of
As pessimistic life, that the end may be
Felicity: ianthine blossoming
           For fitter and unfried scions.

ABERDEEN REVISITED

The gulls laugh madly in the rainy dawn.
Smell of stale fish pervades the railway station –
Indeed, the quays and cobbles and my heart.

Thirty and three years past I sojourned here –
Staggeringly lucky hide-out from the War –
Learning how square waves were to guard old England.

I turn left, have to ask my way: it seems
My *alma mater*'s to the theatre's left.
My tear-filled eyes gaze down a viaduct.

How sad it is about a life that's gone –
Whether about its passing or its mode
Or abdicated ecstasies, who knows?

Yes, I was young and happy here, though bothered
By fate in ways that now seem ludicrous,
And would have guiltily felt blessed to think

More than three decades on I should be searching
For where the Andrew let me live in digs,
And sending postcards to my grand-daughters.

Orderly streets of brownish, greyish stone!
Two drunks – flushed, agitated – stagger past: they were
A little boy and girl in those far days –

Days of impossibly idyllic health;
Days when bad states were doomed, when only guns
Could kill; days that will never come again.

OLD POETS

When Sydney Cockerell told Sassoon how he'd
Told Hardy to give up waxing his moustache,
He laughed his characteristic barking laugh.

I've often thought I ought to shave mine off,
Albeit unwaxed. But plainly I possess
Absurder, more old-fashioned traits my friends

Don't tell me of, though laugh like dogs about.

THE LIFE OF THE BEE

To Allen Tate on his seventy-fifth birthday

Solved: the enigma of the royal egg.
Man has become the master of the bees!
– Though furtively, without their cognizance.

Beyond the wishes of this deity
(Too big to be seen, too alien to be known)
The bees pursue the duty of their race.

– Enact the great mysterious episodes:
The perilous departure of the swarm,
Foundation of the new metropolis,

The nuptial flight, the massacre of males;
And finally return of winter's sleep.
Doesn't it argue an intelligence,

The mere fact bees accept a common life
Yet do their fellow bees the smallest harm
That's possible? They take as some caprice

Of nature events decided by the 'god'.
They are in hands, in fact, quite capable
Of cancelling their race. And yet give us

Advice: 'Watch closely and courageously
Your terrible sorrows, studying them as joys.'
No doubt at all the false god is the human.

The only true divinity is what
We label 'future society'; which bees
Appear to regard more seriously than we.

September going, and my neighbour's bees
Have swapped my dessicated lavender
For the more blushing sedum, where they crawl

Appropriately and yet incongruously
As aircraft landed on the tops of trees.
Their cities – even ours – are still intact,

But only human presidents are mad,
Or murdered by chicanery and cash.
All are born Yankees of the race of men.

Where's our god who will rise above himself?

LAST DREAMS

I.m. Bonamy Dobrée 1891–1974

Sagacious Ella Freeman Sharpe says dreams
Are typical of the human mind and adds:
'The only dreamless state is death.' I note

The place. Again some pages later: 'Our
Essential life knows no mortality.'
The obvious poignard strikes home to the heart.

When I release the walnuts' brainy shells
The husks' insides are as vein-netted as
Our human embryos. And gardening late

(The robin's song like snapping twigs or garden
Chairs being shut, the low sky jaundiced through
The trees), I see such things' nobility.

Each species has its general character –
The dunnock's patient pecking, say, at nothing;
Or human dreams – that conquers special marks.

The father, in the manner of all fathers,
Once brushed the daughter's hair. Time has reversed
The roles. To mark my visit, silver silk

Above the mortal face. I wish I'd said:
'How beautiful you look!' Now it's too late.
In any case, would you have deigned to care?

In those last weeks we used to talk of Tom
And Herbert, best remembered of your friends:
Demotic names, high poets. Gone before you.

'How old am I?' you questioned more than once.
'You're eighty-three,' I said. 'I looked you up.'
You liked it not those months without your wife.

Your life at last seemed almost wholly dreams.
I chose for your committal lines those friends
Would have been sad though scarcely shocked to find

Apt for the grim not ignoble rite:
'From an island of calm a limpid source of love'
And 'Old men ought to be explorers.' It's

The final folding of the summer chair
The robin mimics. Now you can never know
The meaning of the strange recurring dream

In each man's life – one's reason to believe
It's always about some move into a great
And ruined house. Or have you fathomed it?

DEVILISH TIMES

Just bearable, existence for humankind;
And merely by courtesy of the state of play
Between Old Nick and an all too sporting god . . .

The Antagonist was given leave to biff
Everything Job possessed, although discouraged
From destroying the boily patriarch himself . . .

The October evening's almost yellow west.
Black boughs. Black leaves – comparatively few.
A planet's sparkle on the deepening blue.

The last of the watery constellations climbs
Up eastern skies. No wonder we love our verse
Since it's as near our taste as we can make it.

Satan asleep or occupied elsewhere –
For who'd believe that God these devilish times
Tonight was reasserting his rule of good?

The whole cartload of culture starts to jack-knife.
It's the old story. 'So be it,' said the Lord.
'He's in your hands. Though try to spare his life.'

O cosmos, perhaps as beauteous to the mute
As to us vocalists, I dare say you'll
Survive that theological dispute!

– One trusts not too intolerably for ants
Quick under concrete floors; or elephants
Munching across some far away champaign;

Or any creature whose innocence might well
Exempt it from schematic hell – blest state
Both God and poets hope man will attain.

TO GEORGE WOODCOCK, IN HIS AND THE AUTHOR'S SIXTY-FIFTH YEAR

What Marxian spectre lays its beard on the evening?

Lettere dal carcere: yes, but all
Our letters come from prison. In latter days
I'm reading this book by Gramsci, not for ways

To overthrow the wicked bourgeoisie,
Merely to pick up hints for comprehending
Life from a locked-up hunchback's ponderings.

Long since, in war-time, you opposed the war-god –
A stance not quite uncomical. Though now
I might well think: how right! But then it seemed

Evil would only go through evil done.
Besides, the issued arms might in the end
Save us from right-wing maniacs of our own.

As for the past (ongoing!) life of art,
We surely would have never disagreed
On Seneca's epistolary advice:

'Avoid shabby attire, long hair, an unkempt beard;
A known antipathy to knives and forks;
Sleeping on floors; and other misguided means

Of self-advertisement.' I move from book
To tape, the longest trek that, ageing, I want
To take (and you yourself have somewhat cut

Your literally Pacific voyagings);
Hear music that recalls a time before
You and I'd even met: green then my age!

The pianist of that date a friend whose death
Alone proved he'd become more dear: the fiddler,
Widowered, gassed himself at once – odd fate

For someone utterly *moyen sensuel*,
Although response to Bruch's *schmalz* (our own
Not least) must always put us on our guard.

I tie together time and death and art;
Marvel how close to sentimentality
Is art's essential – lasting melody.

O fiddler, dead in what we'd now regard
As youth! O friend, whose age at death we've passed!
In our last decade what fresh insights grow!

From the jail I, and even you, escaped,
Gramsci (about the parcels sent from home)
Complained he didn't get the Cirio

('A brand of marmalade' explains the note).
The nearer we come to losing them, the more
Precious and meaningful the trivia,

So called, of life. The more prolonged the span
Of consciousness the greater homage due
Its fragile vehicle: to cheer the one

Who's lived so long – still more, his friends – by marking
Odd-numbered lustra, wishing him enough
(And lasting) liberty and marmalade;

Fighting to get them if we're also tough.
Gramsci in jail's like us at sixty-five.
'No point in having a new suit made for Court.

'After I'm sentenced I'll be issued with
A proper prisoner's outfit – tunic below
Shaved head. But I agree that folk might say

'My ancient jacket at the trial was
For demogogic show, and so I'll wear
The decent suit I'd kept "for best".' The suit

You and I keep for death and anniversaries.

NOTES

I have kept together, at the end, some poems in three-line stanzas. They were written after my book *From the Joke Shop* (1975) had gone to press, otherwise they would have been part of that sequence. In 'The Life of the Bee' free use is made of Maeterlinck's book with the same title, translated by Alfred Sutro. The italicised line is from Allen Tate's 'To the Lacedemonians'. In the poem 'To George Woodcock' the quotation from Seneca is adapted from Robin Campbell's translation of *Epistulae Morales ad Lucilium* (Penguin Books). The epigraph is from George Woodcock's 'Wartime Evening in Cambridge'. I am not sure I believe the note about 'Cirio' (referred to in the poem) which I think of as a food brand name rather than a specific article of food. It comes in the English translation, *Letters from Prison* (OUP), from which I derive the end of the poem.

In two other poems some material appears with little or no alteration. In 'Saints and Stoics', a notice by Peter Levi of Martin Robertson's *A History of Greek Art*; Banesh Hoffman's *Albert Einstein: Creator and Rebel*; and the anonymous author of a cyclostyled leaflet about St Beuno's Church, Pistyll. In 'The Sloth Moth', a report in *The Times* from Nature-Times News Service, the source being *Science*, July 9, 1976.

When the 'cinquains' were published in *Thames Poetry* (Vol 1, No 3) I prefaced them with a note that the form was invented by the American poet Adelaide Crapsey (1878–1914) and that its rules would be apparent. I too carelessly took the article to be syllable-based, judging from selections in anthologies. Since then Susan Sutton Smith's book on Crapsey (State University of New York Press) has made clear the stress basis of the cinquain. Nevertheless, the inventor's own cinquains do sometimes imply a pause or syllabic count in justification of the one, two, three, four, one-footed lines, so I have not changed things.

OHIO UNIVERSITY LIBRARY

Please return this book as soon as you have finished with it. In order to avoid a fine it must be returned by the latest date stamped below.

CF